DECODING THE SECRET

The Law of Attraction from a Biblical Perspective

By
Rich Cavaness and Leo Schreven

TEACH Services, Inc.
Brushton, New York

2007 08 09 10 11 12 · 5 4 3 2 1

Copyright © 2007 All Power Seminars, Inc.
ISBN-13: 978-1-57258-500-3
ISBN-10: 1-57258-500-5
Library of Congress Control Number: 2007926465

Published by

TEACH Services, Inc.
www.TEACHServices.com

TABLE OF CONTENTS

INTRODUCTION

The purpose of this book is to focus on a topic that is gaining publicity and momentum in the field of self-help, personal development, metaphysics and the new age movement. All the interest and excitement has been generated by the new book and DVD by Rhonda Byrne called **"The Secret."** The materials have sold in the millions and people everywhere are raving about the concepts and principles taught. **"The Secret"** is even being touted as being responsible for helping to usher in "a new ERA for human kind." Major news magazines like 20/20 and Dateline have done broadcasts on the subject. Even well-known talk show hosts Larry King, Ellen DeGeneres and Oprah have gotten on the bandwagon and dedicated entire shows to this topic. Oprah Winfrey herself said on her show that she has been living **"The Secret"** her entire life without even knowing it. In Canada, an entrepreneur and author by the name of Michael J. Losier, has a book titled, "The Law of Attraction" and it is taking Canada by storm! Michael's book is on the top 20 list for Amazon.com as well. But not everyone is convinced. Is all this **"Secret"** stuff really helpful? Or is it a brilliant marketing gimmick playing on Americans' inexhaustible appetite for affirmations, inspirations, and motivations?

Many modern physicists argue with the idea that quantum signals can be perceived on the scale of something like a neuron, a brain, or a human being. The recent Newsweek, March 7 issue, had an article in it by Jerry Adler. He asks, "Is this just the same old stuff marketed in a new way?" and "is this new thought just new marketing?" As a matter of fact, Beryl Satter, a professor of history at Rutgers University, says this same thinking and material existed 100 years ago during the self-help movement of the 19th century!

So why is this momentum building, pseudo-science, physicists based, vibrational frequency, new thought, self-help, such a controversial topic? I believe it is because all these teachers and movie producers are leaving out the most important element: **The Secret is no secret, it's been in the divine writings of the Bible for thousands of years!** The topic has to do with a universal law, an eternal principle set forth by the Creator God of the universe and referred to in the Bible on numerous occasions. **It is the Law of Attraction.** This is not referring to anything regarding your physical beauty or anything of a seductive nature, as the name might lead you to conclude. The **Law of Attraction** has to do with our being a living magnet every moment of our life. **Simply put, you attract into your life, people, situations, circumstances, and experiences that are in harmony with your dominant thoughts.** One of the great universal principles in the Bible comes from **Proverbs 23:7, which says, "For as a man thinks in his heart, so is he."** You become what you think about most of the time!

Everything in your outer world is controlled and brought to life by what's going on in your inner world. What you think about, what you focus on, what you visualize, what you talk to yourself about most of the time, literally becomes your life! **Whatever the mind can conceive and believe, it can achieve.**

So what are your thoughts focusing on most of the time? Can you see that your life experiences are really just a mirror, a reflection of those thoughts and images in your mind? I believe that **attention +**

intention + belief = the creation of things! Thoughts really do become things we can touch, feel, taste, and smell. What many do not realize is that the very essence of **"The Secret"** is condensed into three words of Jesus Christ: **Ask, Believe, and Receive.**

Most people really struggle with this aspect of the **Law of Attraction.** The reality is that your life right now, your circumstances right now, your challenges right now, are the sole result of the dominant thoughts of your conscious and subconscious mind. What you do or do not do is a direct result of your thinking patterns. Most people are focusing on today—their lack, their current situation, their big challenges, the things of their past, instead of focusing on abundant life, what they really want and how their life will be when they reach their goals.

One of our great concerns today is the trend in this **"new thought"** arena which is heavily connected to the New Age Movement and channeling. It's really an amalgamation of many different religions and beliefs rolled up into one splendid "get what you want" package! An individual who has been very involved in **"The Secret"** movie, and subsequent interviews, has been entrepreneur and spiritual teacher, James Ray. For over two decades, he has been a well-known motivational speaker and personal coach. James Ray says this about **"The Secret"**:

"The Secret is about supporting the great spiritual traditions in a more modern form. It's really just putting Christianity, Judaism, all the great teachings into a current vernacular."

The current popular teachings of the law of attraction have much validity and powerful concepts to them. However, it is often without any Creator-God or Biblical perspective. I have read numerous books and articles on this topic but 99% of them do not have a Bible perspective which we believe sheds a different light on the subject. You see, the Bible teaches that God wants to answer your prayers. God wants you to be living an abundant and prosperous life. God wants you to think positive and faith affirming thoughts. These are well established facts and principles that are taught in the Bible. So on this basis **The Law of Attraction is a very solid Biblical teaching!** You will see this very clearly in this book. This book is designed and intended to take an open and honest look at the topic of the **Law of Attraction from a Godly standpoint** and at the same time point out some of the current teachings and directions, that can be dangerous and lead people astray. Many of you are living an average and mediocre life. Some of you are in a rut. Some of you feel that nothing ever goes right in your life. Whether you believe it or not, whether you acknowledge it or not, the **Law of Attraction** is affecting you and having an influence on your life. May this book open up the windows of Heaven to you in your emotional, physical, financial, mental, and relational aspects of your life.

Rich Cavaness,
President and Speaker of All Power Ministries

Chapter 1

THE EIGHT UNIVERSAL LAWS OF THE MIND

Let's start out by asking some challenging and thought provoking questions. Please give careful and meditative thought to each of them:

Why is it that some people are more successful than others?

Why is it that some sales people are more successful than others?

Why is it that some business owners are more successful than others?

Why is it that some entrepreneurs are more successful than others?

In conducting personal development and motivational seminars, pastoral and evangelism ministry classes, and business entrepreneur training worldwide, here is what we have discovered:

- The difference between the high achiever and those who settle for mediocrity,
- the difference between happiness and depression,
- the difference between successful and prosperous people and those who settle for failure and lack,
- the difference between those people who live healthy, abundant physical lives and those who are constantly sick and diseased,

- the difference between those who are in good relationships and those who are not in good relationships is **one thing:**

One group understands the laws of the mind, how the mind works, and how to cooperate with the fixed laws God has given us as men and women made in the image of God. This automatically leads them to success and blessings. The other group constantly break these laws and reap the painful consequences.

There are eight basic laws. These laws explain why some people have wonderful, abundant, happy lives and others do not. So lets take a look at each of the eight mental laws and discover together what they are and how they apply to our lives.

Some of the laws may appear to be very similar in nature, and they are. But each one of them has a unique function in the outcomes of your life and the place and circumstances of your life today as you are reading this. **The eight mental laws of the mind** are as follows:

The Law of Cause and Effect
The Law of Control
The Law of Belief
The Law of Expectations
The Law of Attraction
The Law of Concentration
The Law of Sub-Conscious Activity
The Law of Correspondence

The Law of Cause and Effect

This law states that for every cause, there is a direct effect! Everything happens for a reason. This means nothing happens by accident, by chance, or by luck. It's a matter of law! Even if you do not know the reason something happens, there is still a reason that explains it. You see, the Bible teaches the principle that success leaves clues! **Galatians 6:7–8, "Don't be misled: No one makes a fool of God. What a person plants, he will harvest. The person who plants selfishness, ignoring the needs of others, will harvest a crop of weeds. All they will have to show for their life is weeds! But the one who plants in response to God, letting God's Spirit do the growth work in him, harvests a crop of real life, eternal life."**

What you sow, you will reap! For every cause there is an effect, either positive or negative. One of the best ways to insure your outcomes in life is to role-model other successful and productive individuals. If you follow in their path, following their actions and teachings, you will eventually get the same results. For the Christian, the Bible teaches us that Jesus Christ is our role model. The results are we become like Him. It is the same in every area of life. If you really want to be healthy, happy, prosperous, popular, positive, and confident, find out how people who are enjoying these benefits got that way then do the same things that they do. Think the same thoughts, feel the same feelings, take the same actions, and eventually you will get the same results as they do.

The Law of Control

This law says that you will feel happy to the degree with which you feel you are in control of your own life. I think most of us can relate to this law, because the reverse is true as well. We will feel unhappy to the degree with which we feel we out of control of our own life. The Bible tells us that God is not a God of confusion or chaos. That tells me that our lives shouldn't be that way either. This is where you either accept responsibility for your life, or you become a victim. You are a free moral agent. You make your own choices and decisions in your life. You are either confident, happy, and courageous, or you can be a victim and allow your life to be controlled by others. Most people are not in control at all. They are controlled by the fast food industry, the beverage industry, the music and movie industry, the fashion industry, the credit card industry, the sports industry, the advertising industry, and the anti-God industry. **The question is, "Which industry controls you?"**

The Law of Belief

This law states that whatever you believe with conviction becomes your reality. The Bible, of all books on planet earth, teaches the importance of our beliefs. As a matter of fact the word "belief" is found hundreds of times in the Bible along with some great illustrations of its importance. **Proverbs 23:7 says, "That as a man thinks in his heart, that is what he becomes." In Mark 9:23 the Bible says, "If you can believe, all things are possible to them who believe." Jesus Christ Himself said this about belief in Matthew 9 and 15, "According to your faith it will be done to you." And "Dear woman, you really do have a lot of faith, and you will be given what you want."**

One thing I have discovered about the word belief is that people do not believe what they see, they actually see what they already believe! So let's define what a belief actually is.

A belief is a feeling of certainty about something, whether it's true or false. It is developed by the many references in your life you have used to establish it.

You see, you can develop beliefs about anything if you find enough references in your life to establish it in your mind. Your beliefs affect everything in your life. Some of these beliefs are good, but many are not and they are very destructive in our lives. Often a single experience in our past creates a negative belief that we carry through our life, even if its not true! The truth is that most of our beliefs are generalizations about our past, based on our perceptions of the pain or pleasure our experiences cause. Most of us underestimate the power of our beliefs.

Here's how it works. Once a belief is accepted, your belief becomes an unquestioned command to your nervous system. Then that belief has the power to increase or limit the possibilities of your life! Beliefs have the power to create and they have the power to destroy. Our Creator God has given us the awesome ability to take any experience in our life, and create a meaning for it, and that meaning can either destroy your life, or it can create a meaning that will literally save and enrich your life. In taking your life to the next level of personal success, one of the key steps will be to challenge your limiting and disempowering beliefs. Please never forget this important point, the only limitations you have in your life are those you place on yourself!

The Law of Expectations

This law states that whatever you expect with confidence, becomes your own self-fulfilling prophecy. Your ideas, visions, and dreams, whatever they may be, are the prophecies of what one day you shall become and achieve. You see, you do not necessarily get what you want in life, but you will always get what you expect! If you confidently expect something to happen, this expectation has a powerful effect on your attitude—your personality. The more confident you are in your expectations of something happening in your life, the more likely you will say and do the things that are consistent with what you expect to happen. Plain and simple—successful and high achieving people expect in advance to be successful, high achievers. It's not something that just happens, they expect it to happen, therefore it does! The result of these high and positive expectations is that it significantly increases the probabilities that you will achieve exactly what you are wanting in your life. You see, when you think, breathe, expect, and visualize success, then it happens for you. The other side of this is simple to observe. Let's take the average American for example. They get up, go to work, go in debt, pay taxes, watch 20 hours of TV each week, and start that routine the next day all over again. Most have no expectations and are satisfied with just getting by. The highlight of their day is to just survive. Did you ever notice that people always get what they expect?

The Law of Attraction

This law states that you are a living magnet. You attract into your life people, circumstances, situations that are in harmony with your dominant thoughts. One of the most important habits that you can establish in your life is to keep your mind full of exciting, positive, and emotionally charged pictures and images of the exact things you want to see materialize in your life and in the world around you. This law is more powerful than we could ever begin to imagine.

The Law of Concentration

This law states that whatever you dwell upon, grows and expands in your life. Simply put, whatever you think about most of the time increases. More and more of your mental energies and emotions become focused and concentrated on what you are dwelling upon. Focusing more of your mental energy and thoughts on goal attainment helps you move toward them faster. Successful people focus and concentrate their energy and time on what it is in life they want, and the not-so-surprising result is they usually get it! **People who fail in life are usually focusing on what they don't want, and they usually get it too.**

The Law of Subconscious Activity

This law states that your subconscious mind accepts any thought, plan, or goal created by the conscious mind and then organizes your thoughts and behaviors to bring that goal into reality. Whatever thoughts, goals, or actions you repeat over and over again in your conscious mind are eventually accepted by your subconscious mind. Your subconscious mind then goes to work, 24/7, to coordinate your thoughts, goals, dreams, words, and actions to bring these into your life. That is why it is so important to be careful what you put into your mind. Before you go to bed at night fill your mind with positive things like the Bible, a positive book, affirmations, goals, or tomorrow's actions. Your mind even while sleeping is at work to bring into reality what you put into it, whether it's good or bad.

The Law of Correspondence

This law simply states that your outer world is a reflection of your inner world. Without exception and in every case, your outer world reflects back to you, like a mirror image, exactly what you are thinking in the deepest recesses of your mind. The way you treat people, the way you think about your physical body, the way you think about money and your finances, the way you think about your job or career, will all be reflected back to you in your personal life.

When you take these eight great mental laws of the mind and summarize them, you come up with one, great universal principle that explains your life and everything that happens to you...

YOU BECOME WHAT YOU THINK ABOUT MOST OF THE TIME!

That means you move in the direction of your dominant thoughts. Everything in your outer world is controlled and determined by what you are thinking in your inner world.

There is only one thing in the entire universe that you actually have 100% complete control over. **Your mind.** Not even God will do this for you. God tells you what to do, and how, but ultimately the choice is yours. You are the one who determines what you think about most of the time. So the great news is that by taking complete responsibility and control of your conscious mind and thoughts, you can literally control the direction of your life. You can live a life of all power and no limits. You can become unstoppable. You can achieve your life's dreams, you can be whatever you want to be! The only thing that will ever hold you back or place limits on your life, is you! **John D. Rockefeller once said, "If a man thinks he can or not, then he is probably right."**

Chapter 2

THE BIBLICAL AND SCIENTIFIC TRUTH OF "THE SECRET"

Both of us consider ourselves to be very open-minded people. We are open to new and exciting ideas, we love to think outside the traditional boundaries of how things are being done, and we really enjoy looking at how we can improve or make things better that are already in place. We believe in 95% of the basic tenets of what **"The Secret"** is all about. Here is a basic outline of **"The Secret"** teachings that are in alignment with Bible principles, science, and medical research:

We all work with one infinite power. The Bible teaches there is one true God, the Creator God of the Universe. He is above all other Gods. The one distinguishing characteristic that separates the God of the Bible from any other God, from all ancient spiritual beings, or religious leaders, is that the one true God, the living God, has made the heavens, the earth, and everything above and below. **Jeremiah 10:10–13 and Revelation 4:11 make this clear.**

Learn to become still and have daily quiet times. We live in a very busy and 24/7 geared society and many have challenges slowing down the pace of life. Quiet time everyday can be so beneficial, because how you begin each day can set the tone for your entire day. God says to us, **"Be still and know that I am God."** Some of you may refer to this as meditation, some may refer to this as just being still and listening for God's voice, while others may see this as going for a nice walk in God's creation. We recommend taking 15–20 minutes at the beginning of each day, to reflect, be still, pray, listen, and engage the Creator God. **Psalm 4:3–5 and Philippians 4:8 teach this principle.**

Our Lives are meant to be abundant in all areas—the physical, mental, emotional, spiritual, financial, and relational. The word **"abundance"** refers to a plentiful supply. We believe and teach that God wants His people, His children to rise above mediocrity and to be the light and example to the world. The Bible tells us that God wants His joy to remain in us and that our joy would be full and overflowing! **John 10:10 and 3 John 2** tells us that God came to give us abundant life, and even goes so far as to say that *above all things* God wants us to prosper and be in health. **So the gospel of prosperity is 100% Biblical!** We know there are some organizations that have taken this out of context and taught unbiblical principles. We need to be careful though, not to throw the baby out with the bathwater. God's original plan for Israel was that they would so closely follow his principles that they would be the head in all the world and would acknowledge that following God's ways brings great blessings. Too often we are content to be the tail, not the head.

We are like living magnets—we become who and what we associate with. The Bible supports this fact. What and how we think in our minds, tends to become reality in our lives! What we fix our minds on, tends to be what we attract more of in our life. That's why the Bible tells us that where you treasure is, your heart will be also! Treasure is not just material things, but thoughts of your heart, whatever you think about most, whatever may be a priority or motive for you. **Proverbs 23:7 and 2 Corinthians 3:18**

Whatever the mind can conceive and believe, it can achieve!

Choose your thoughts carefully, your dominant thoughts become your reality, whether good or bad. Your thoughts will dictate the course of your life, either to great levels of success and high achievement or they will keep you stuck in the rut of life. The great news is that you can control what goes into your mind, what influences your mind, and thus can have your thoughts propel you to greatness! **Jesus Christ in Matthew 17:20 said, "If you have faith as a grain of mustard seed, you will say to this mountain , move from here to there, it will move; nothing shall be impossible for you."** Do you believe that?

If you want to live the life of your dreams, then you have to decide what it is you desire from your life. Think and strive for what you want by setting goals and creating visual images such as dream boards. **Proverbs 29:18 tells us "Without a vision the people perish."** Without dreams we may not die physically, but we'll definitely be dead in every other area of life. Have a reason to get out of bed in the mornings, have a purpose and a crusade bigger than yourself. Life will become whatever you want it to be. You can't hit a target unless you know where it is. Because most people never decide what they really want in their life physically, mentally, spiritually, emotionally or financially they end up settling for far less than they are capable of achieving. This is one of the greatest tragedies in humanity today.

There is power in our words! Words are the outward manifestations of our thoughts. So what you speak of most frequently, you get more of in your life. The Bible tells us our words can either be like poison or honey, they can either build up or tear down. Words have the power to speak your future destination and outcome of your life. **Did you know that a positive, affirming thought and word, is 100 times more powerful than a negative one?** Look for the miracle that is in your mouth. **Proverbs 16:24, Matthew 15:8–11 and James 3:5–12**

Too much time is spent on worry, fear, anxiety, and feelings of having to control everyone and everything. When we pray or ask God for our wants, we need to trust Him to see the situation the best way. Give up control and wanting to know the "how" and just trust in God to provide the answers. When you have belief and faith, God moves mightily. **Proverbs 3:5–6**

God has given us the power of choice so we can create our own world. We cannot change the whole world, but we <u>can</u> change our world! By accepting responsibility for our lives, our decisions, and the direction of our life, we can then have the personal power to live a life of no limits! You can literally become the master architect of your life. That's the amazing thing about the Creator God—He allows us to choose to love or not to love; to forgive or not to forgive; to be Bible believing people or to be world believing people; to use our God given talents and abilities to bless others or to use them for selfish and greedy gain. We can even choose whether to love Him or not! **Joshua 24:14–15 and Deuteronomy 11:26–28**

Thoughts cause feelings and your feelings can determine your attitude, your emotional states, and the outcomes of your life. By changing your emotional state, you can literally change the direction of your life. How you walk, talk, your posture, the speed at which you go about life, your smile, and your words, can have a great impact on your emotions and feelings. Whatever it is you are feeling, is a perfect reflection of what is becoming your life. The Bible tells us that a positive and happy attitude will help us smile more and that living a life of faith, belief, and optimism is like having a great party with our family and friends everyday. **Proverbs 15:13, 15 and Proverbs 17:22**

Most people are dedicating too much thought and energy to "What-Is" which is their current situation in life, rather than what they want their life to be like. Albert Einstein once said, "The definition of insanity is doing the same thing over and over again and expecting to get different results." Your life is full of possibilities. Focus on those and the kind of life you really want to live. If you want things to be different, then you need to be motivated to change and apply the principles of success in your life. **Proverbs 23:7**

It is absolutely critical to begin each day with an attitude of gratitude! Be thankful for everything God has blessed you with.

Everything in your life is a blessing, everything! From all of it we learn, we grow, and we expand our life for the better— the mountain top experiences and the death valley experiences.

The Bible tells us that all things work together for good, for them that love God. It's going to be very hard for God to bless and give you more of what you want in your life if you're not happy with what you currently have. Today our society is filled with too much whining and complaining, we need to be more thankful because we are all blessed. **Psalm 95:2 and Philippians 4:6–7**

See yourself with great value and worth. Respect yourself and the people around you as a special creation from God. Most people today are trying to please others, make more money, and work hard at pleasing God. Their entire worth and value is wrapped up in "doing" and not "being". Your value and worth in God's eyes is not about what you do or don't do. It's about who you are on the inside. The Bible teaches us to love one another, to forgive one another, and to treat others as we want to be treated. One of the great tenets of success is the higher your self-esteem and self-worth, the higher you can go up the ladder of success and achievement. This is why Jesus taught, "Love your neighbor as you love yourself." Do you love yourself? Most people hate themselves or have a low self-esteem. When you understand that you were made in the very image and likeness of God, then you will see that God sees great value and worth in you. **Genesis 1: 26–28, Genesis 2:7, and Jeremiah 33:3**

Our daily habits will determine the outcomes of our lives. If they are good and empowering habits, then they will move you toward feeling good and drive you toward goal accomplishment. If they are limiting and disempowering habits, then they will keep you living an average life of mediocrity. Daily habits can make or break a person.

When the doors of opportunity open before you, take action and just do it! Too many are allowing procrastination and fear to control their lives. Information and knowledge are important and needed, but only when they are applied and lived out do they really make us powerful and successful. We see too many people today waiting around for some magic moment or a lightning bolt from heaven to strike before they make the decision to act. People are waiting for God to do all the work or open all the doors. This is where faith and action join together. Yes, we need to be open and attentive to God's voice. We do this while we are moving forward and pressing toward the direction we sense and feel God is leading. **James 2:14–26**

From a physical standpoint, many people are making decisions today to live a sick and diseased life. They are not providing the body what it needs to be a healing agent. From the writings of Plato and Galen, we see there is such a strong connection between the mind and the body and the health and wellness of a person. Plato said this, "The cure for many diseases is unknown to physicians because they are ignorant of the whole. For the part can never be well unless the whole is well." When we are strong physically, then we can be strong in our minds. With a positive attitude, a smile, laughing, reducing stress, and enjoying life, we can greatly enhance the immune system of our bodies to help us live healthy and strong. **Science has proven that 90% of all sickness and disease in our world today is there because of what we are doing to ourselves.** When it comes to our lifestyles and health, it's not a matter of chance, it's a matter of choice!

In regard to cancer, Harold H. Benjamin, PhD, makes this powerful comment, "Laughter in and of itself cannot cure cancer nor prevent cancer, but laughter as part of the full range of positive emotions including hope, love, faith, strong will to live, determination, and purpose, can be a significant and indispensable aspect of the total fight for recovery." Several studies have shown that a positive attitude or emotional state can boost your chances of surviving cancer. The late Norman Cousins, an oncologist at the UCLA Medical School, in his book, "Head First: The Biology of Hope" told of conducting a national survey of 649 oncologists regarding the various psychological factors in fighting cancer. The results were surprising—it wasn't drugs, chemo, and radiation that made the biggest difference, it was a patient's attitude of hope and optimism.

Hope is the emotional and mental state that motivates you to keep on living, to accomplish great things and succeed. With hope, a positive attitude can be maintained, determination can be strengthened, coping skills sharpened, and love and support more freely given and received. Researchers today are now experimenting and creating a new field related to the combat of cancer called psychoneuroimmunology. This study focuses on such techniques as meditation, biofeedback, and visualization. In our experience, people thrive in life when they have a positive will to live. This means they really want to live. They want to enjoy life, they want to get every ounce of juice out of life, and they believe that their life has meaning and purpose to it. The Bible truly supports these findings. As a matter of fact, many of the great healings that Jesus Christ conducted during His life were based on the person's faith or belief that they could be healed by Him.

We believe the key is to take care of your physical body now and treat it like the creation of God that it is. Then couple that with attitude, faith, belief, hope, self-control, determination and fun, and many of the diseases and ailments of our day will not be part of your life. **Proverbs 17:22, Matthew 9:29, 17:16–20 and 1 Corinthians 10:31**

Wealth and prosperity are the result of a proper mindset. Steven Forbes recently made an amazing statement on Fox News about wealth creation. "The real source of wealth and capital is not material things, it is the human mind, the human spirit, the human imagination, and our faith in the future. The magic of a free society is that everyone can move forward and prosper because **wealth comes from within!"**

Remember, the Bible teaches that what you think in your mind becomes your physical reality. So if you have negative thinking in regard to money, being rich, being financially blessed, and living a life of abundance and prosperity, then that determines in your life whether money is your friend or your foe. A person's verbal programming, the models they have seen, and specific incidents that have happened will determine whether money affects them in a positive or negative way. Most people today, including Christians, have not really done an exhaustive study in the Bible about what God really says and thinks about being prosperous and rich financially. The Bible as a whole clearly teaches the principles of financial abundance.

The Bible has over 2,350 references to money and possessions in it. Out of the 38 parables that Jesus taught, 16 of them deal directly with how we handle money! In the New Testament alone, 1 out of every 10 verses is speaking about money and possessions. Even Jesus Himself spoke more about money than Heaven and hell combined!

In Psalm 112:1–3 the Bible says, "Praise the Lord. Blessed is the man who fears the Lord, who finds great delight in His commands. His children will be mighty in the land; each generation of the upright will be blessed. <u>Wealth and riches</u> are in his house, and his righteousness endures forever." The wisest man who ever lived, Solomon, says this about work, wealth, and enjoying the fruits of our labor in **Proverbs 3:16, "Wisdom gives: A long, good life, <u>riches</u>, honor, pleasure, and peace."**

Ecclesiastes 5:18–19, "Then I realized that it is good and proper for a man to eat and drink, and to

find satisfaction in his toilsome labor under the sun during the few days of life God has given him, for this is his lot in life. Moreover, when <u>God gives any man wealth and possessions</u>, and enables him to enjoy them, to accept his lot and be happy in his work, this is the gift of God." There are so many positive verses in the Bible on this subject.

You see, the issue in the Bible is about **your mindset, the motives of your heart, and what you do with what you gain.** We believe the Bible teaches three distinct laws when it comes to money.

The first law is the law of ownership. God owns everything.

Psalm 24:1 says, "The earth is the Lord's, and all its fullness, the world and those who dwell in it."

Haggai 2:8 says, "The silver is Mine, and the gold is Mine, says the Lord."

Deuteronomy 8:18 says, "Always remember that it is the <u>Lord your God</u> who gives you power to become rich."

The second law is the law of stewardship.

1 Corinthians 4:1 says, "Let man so account of us, as ministers of Christ, and <u>stewards</u> of the mysteries of God. Moreover it is required in <u>stewards</u> that a man be found faithful."

The job of a steward is to oversee that which belongs to someone else. In this case, God's money. We are stewards of God's money.

Two more important aspects of stewardship are your work ethic and saving money. Creating wealth and prosperity takes planning and working diligently at it. In the real world there is not such thing as "get rich quick." Those things come and go. We are talking about putting "sweat equity" into your business and financial endeavors. Notice what the Bible says about this in **Proverbs 12:24, "Work hard and** become a leader, by lazy and never succeed." Proverbs 14:23 says, "Work brings profit; talk brings poverty." And in Proverbs 28:19 it says, "Hard work brings prosperity; playing around brings poverty."

Americans today are the worst at saving money. We now have the highest percentage of people living paycheck to paycheck in the world! 1 out of 4 Americans say they don't have any spare cash. The average personal savings rate is now less than 2% of income earned. According to the Bible it should not be this way.

Proverbs 21:20 says, "The wise man saves for the future, but the foolish man spends whatever he gets." And in Proverbs 13:22 it says, "When a good man dies he leaves an inheritance to his grandchildren."

Plain and simple: The Bible teaches the necessity of work, the importance of giving to others, the need for savings, and the power of accountability and responsibility in how you manage your money.

The third law is servant hood.

1 Corinthians 7:22 says, "For he who is called in the Lord while a <u>servant</u>, is the Lord's freeman. Likewise he who is called while free is Christ's servant."

A servant does what his master says. So, we are to do what God says and follow His biblical principles.

When we follow these three laws regarding money we never go wrong.

The Bible promotes prosperity, working hard, building wealth and investing, making your money grow, giving and helping others in need. The key to acknowledgment on our part is who really owns wealth and how we are stewards of it. There is a danger in this and God spells it out in **Deuteronomy**

8:18, **"Always remember that it is the <u>Lord your God</u> <u>who gives you power to become rich...</u>"**

Another important point we want to make here is that there is a difference between being wealthy and being rich. We believe in teaching people about financial freedom and the Bible principles of financial wealth. But we also believe in helping people to be wealthy in every area of their lives—physical, emotional, and mental wealth; financial, spiritual, and relationship wealth. It all goes together. We have met lots of people who are rich financially but their relationships are a disaster. That's not wealth! We have met people who are spiritually fit but are sick, broke, and in debt. That's not wealth either! We have met people who are fit, athletic, and healthy physically, but are emotionally and mentally a basket case. That's not wealth! Life is meant to be abundant in every single area of who we are. Happiness is not guaranteed and doesn't happen by going after the material things of the world. Happiness and material things come when we are balanced, running on all our cylinders, have inner peace, know our purpose, and have the right mindset. Money and financial abundance comes when our inward person is in alignment with our values, our money blueprint, our behavior, and our goals.

So there you have it, **17 principles** from **"The Secret"** that we can see from the Bible, medical and science arenas. Now as we go to the next chapter, we are going to discuss with you some major issues and challenges from a Bible perspective with some of **"The Secret"** teachings.

Chapter 3

THE BIBLICAL AND SCIENTIFIC CHALLENGES OF "THE SECRET"

One of the most damaging and major flaws in **"The Secret"** is the belief that the "Universe" and "Energy" are responsible for **the Law of Attraction in our lives. The whole premise is that we are mass energy, that we are infinite beings, and that the Universe gives us whatever we ask for.** This teaching is flawed because the Creator and Maker of energy, the Creator of the universe, the earth, and you and me, are taken totally out of the equation. We acknowledge the components of energy and its powers. We acknowledge the vastness and awesomeness of the universe we live in. We acknowledge the amazing capacity and power we have in our minds to create and accomplish amazing things. But where we draw the line is the fact that the Creator God of the Universe, the God of the Bible, has made it all. So instead of giving thought and prayer to the universe, instead of relying on some energy source within us or outside us, instead of relying on ancient teachers or spirits from the past, we go right to the source! **All energy and power come from God, plain and simple.** One of the major themes in the Bible is to worship Him who made the heavens, the earth, the seas, and fountains of waters. Everything below and above the earth, was made by Him. From Genesis to Revelation, this thread of truth runs consistently through the Bible. **Genesis 1 and 2, Job 38, Psalm 33:6–9, Isaiah 40:21–29, Jeremiah 10:10–13, Revelation 14:7**

We are mass energy and all our thoughts have a frequency and send out magnetic energy. First of all, the Bible states plainly what we are made of. In Genesis 2:7, it says that you and I are made from the dust of the earth. I remember listening to the music group Kansas, who had a song entitled, "Dust in the Wind". The main lyrics said, "All we are is dust in the wind." Another picture the Bible gives about our physical existence compares us to a vapor. Psalm 39:5 says this, "Certainly every man at his best state is but vapor."

The next thing we need to realize is there are different levels of scientists. There are those who are mainstream on most topics. Next, there are those who are making breakthroughs and are not always part of the mainstream belief or proof. And then there are those who are on the "fringes" of mainstream science, like you hear on Coast to Coast AM radio. It is important to understand that some of the science presented on **"The Secret"** DVD movie and from other Law of Attraction authors, seems to be not only on the fringe but bordering on the absurd. One of the concepts of **"The Secret"** that is very misleading is that the **Law of Attraction** works in some magical way or form, and that you can manipulate objective physical reality. You look at something, then the next thing you know it shows up out of nowhere! Don't get us wrong—as we have stated clearly, your thinking plays a huge role in your ability to be successful or not. We believe that success leaves clues! But it involves educating the mind, focusing, planning, failing from time to time, perseverance and persistence, goals, and attaining the tools to apply the principles of success. This can happen relatively fast, but for most people, this will not happen overnight. Most physicists will readily admit today to the idea that quantum signals can be perceived on the scale of something like a neuron. Quantum signals on the brain, or a human being are remote at best. Most scientists will tell you that the effects are tiny, on the order of a few hundredths of 1%! So the idea that you can look at a necklace or a watch and it will leap onto your body, or that as you go to a car showroom and look at a BMW, it will suddenly appear in your driveway, is really beyond the scope of true physics. Do the dominant thoughts and images we hold in our minds have power? Absolutely! But there needs to be action on your part, there needs to be a plan to make it happen. That's why we are against teaching and being part of get-rich-quick ideas, because that is not normal nor Biblical.

The Secret is the Law of Attraction. The unfortunate ruth in all this is that what's been solid Bible principles now for thousands of years has become in recent years more of a "secret" to most Christian believers. The concept of **Ask, Believe, and Receive** is spoken of by **Jesus Himself!** The concept of whatever you think about most often, that's what you become is taught **in Proverbs.** The concepts of whatever you focus on with your eyes and ears goes into your mind and you begin to exhibit the physical equivalent is taught by **the Apostle Paul in Philippians and Corinthians.** The concept of living with intention, which is really expectancy, like faith and belief, this teaching is the **very foundation of the Christian faith!**

So as far as **"The Secret"** being only known by such people as Plato, Shakespeare, Newton, Hugo, Beethoven, Lincoln, Emerson, Edison, Einstein, Buddha, Churchill, Bell, Bollier, Holmes, Jung, Wattles, and Ford, this is really not accurate. They educated themselves in the principles of success, and the **Law of Attraction** became a positive and powerful tool for them to accomplish great things in their lives. But it's just like anything else in life, the truth has always been there in the Bible—people have just chosen not to read it or accept it. We believe people just haven't been fully educated on how to apply these Bible principles.

The universe is an inexhaustible storehouse of goodies from which you command whatever you desire. My first thought when I heard Rhonda Byrne say this was, "If it's that easy, why are not more people getting what they ask for?" That reminds me of a scene I saw from the movie "Bruce Almighty" where Jim Carey gets to play God for a short period of time. All these prayers are coming to him, so he gets on the Yahweh email system, and hits "Yes" to all the prayer requests. The world went crazy. Millions of people won the lottery, people lost weight on the donut hole diet, men didn't need Viagra anymore, it was total chaos!

The reason being most people have no clue what they **REALLY** want out of life. Think about it, if God just granted to everyone anything and everything they requested of Him, then what lessons would there be to learn in life? The Bible says several things are necessary for us to have our prayers answered: We need to be connected and in a relationship with God. We need to have our lives in alignment with His values and principles in the Bible. And we claim the Holy Spirit to be given to guide and direct us to follow God's principles in our lives. I personally know of hundreds of people who ask God to bless them with a lottery win, or some publisher's clearing house sweepstakes, or some expensive car or exotic vacation drawing, and yet they do not win or receive the prize. **WHY?** They have not educated themselves far enough yet to have God really give them their request. Their minds are not prepared, nor are they mentally and emotionally ready. For example, most people cannot handle large sums of money because they are not good stewards of what they already have. Their view of money and their mindset are not mature enough. It takes effort, skills, a plan, and education to make money work for you instead of you working for it.

The other reason is that often times people are praying about things that are clearly spelled out in the Bible. So by praying or asking God for more enlightenment or to open up more doors or avenues of understanding when it is plainly spelled out in the Bible, is like telling God you aren't ready for that in your life. God is the one who knows the right time and place to answer your prayer. **Matthew 7:7, Luke 11:13, John 15:7, 1John 5:15**

Everything in your life you have attracted! This is one area that has caused many people to misunderstand the Law of Attraction. When it comes to concentration camps, genocide, tsunamis, earthquakes, tornados, hurricanes, terrorist attacks, can it really be possible, as **"The Secret"** implies, that people brought that fate down upon themselves? Rhonda Byrne was asked about someone getting pushed off a building or beaten with a club or axed to death during a bout of ethnic cleansing. She replied, **"The Law of Attraction is that each one of us is determining the frequency that we're on by what we're thinking and feeling. If we are in fear, if we're feeling in our lives that we're victims and feeling powerless, then we are on a frequency of attracting those things to us. Totally unconsciously, totally innocently, totally all of those words that are so important."**

From a Biblical perspective here is a more simple explanation. We live in a world that is cursed because of sin. Sin is the great destroyer of success, families, happiness, and all that is good. There is a battle being waged in our universe, it's the battle between good and evil, the battle between Jesus Christ the righteous, and Satan the destroyer. Have you ever asked these questions:

Why do bad things happen to good people? Why do accidents occur when it seems we were just in the wrong place at the wrong time? Why is there pain, death, suffering, and deplorable conditions on the earth today? The answer: SIN!

When the world rebels against God and His principles of right and wrong, His value system, and His truth, then you have a world that has these things happening all the time.

Ephesians 6:12 states this clearly: **"For we do not wrestle against flesh and blood, but against principalities, against powers, against the rulers of the darkness of this age, against spiritual hosts of wickedness in the heavenly places."** In **Revelation 12:7,** the Bible tells us there was a war in heaven and that God cast down to this earth 1/3 of all the created angels along with Lucifer, who then became Satan. Then when you read Genesis Chapters 2–3, you see how this whole mess got started down here! Thankfully, God has a solution and sent His own son Jesus Christ to live a perfect life and give us a model to follow. God gave a solution to the result of sin which is death. Jesus took your penalty, He took your place, so you could have forgiveness of sin and live for eternity in Heaven. To some of you this may be the real **"secret"** you have been waiting to hear. God loves you, God has a plan for you, and God wants you to live with Him throughout eternity. So the missing secret of **"The Secret"** is that this life is just temporary, the real life to come is the one that counts—**your eternal life.**

When you have an inspired thought, you must trust it. Good feelings mean you are on the right track and bad feelings mean you are on the wrong track. It can be dangerous to live your life 100% dependent on your feelings. Just because something feels good, doesn't necessarily make it right or responsible. I believe people who are clear on life roles, values, personal mission, goals, and spiritual beliefs, rely less on feelings and more on their inner compass of who they are and what they stand for and believe. Remember, the subconscious mind can bring anything up to your conscious mind at anytime. All our thoughts cannot be inspired, all our thoughts are not always good. That's why we need to continually ground ourselves in the word of God. True faith comes when we trust God at His word; if God's word says it, then that's good enough for me! That is something solid you can stand on, not just some emotion or feeling. God's word is like His universal Global Positioning System (GPS) to us. If we follow His directions we will not get lost. Biblical principles always work. They are our guides for life. They make your life, health, relationships, finances, emotions, and everything better.

The pro's and con's of "The Secret" have been done in love and we hope it has been an education for you. We encourage you to go through the Bible for yourself and look up the texts given to make sure you understand the principles and ideas we have taught.

The Biblical perspective gives an edge missing in "The Secret" and if you apply it, it can make all the difference in your life and success.

Chapter 4

THE CREATOR GOD OF THE UNIVERSE

The Law of Attraction is such a universal principle of life, that whether you know it or not, it is affecting your life either in a positive way or a negative way. Many success and personal development teachers and coaches today teach this principle in their seminars and to their students and clients. One of the great dangers I see is this trend of teaching the Law of Attraction but without a Godly or Bible-based perspective. That's one of the great challenges we see with **"The Secret"** material.

There are a number of individuals who are writing books and articles, making movies, like the new **"The Secret"** movie, and creating DVDs and CDs on the subject. They are genuinely educating and helping people improve their lives, but from our perspective there is a key element being left out in the universal principle of the Law of Attraction. That is what we want to address. So let's spend some time together learning and understanding the Biblical perspective to the Law of Attraction.

The Bible teaches clearly that God has a plan, a purpose, and a reason for creating every single individual here on planet earth. You see, you are not here by mistake or by some chance event, by a freak accident or by some billion-year evolutionary process. You were made in the image and likeness of the Creator God of the universe! God wants all of us to experience joy, love, appreciation, passion, happiness, optimism, hope, peace, prosperity, and a life filled with abundance in every aspect. As a matter of fact the Bible says this in **John 10:10, "I have come that they may have life, more and better life than they ever dreamed of."** And in **3 John 2 the Bible says, "I pray for your good fortune in everything you do, and for your good health, that your everyday affairs prosper, as well as your soul!"** God's plan and desire for us is to have the life of our dreams, to accomplish goals, to reach for the stars with all the talents and abilities He has given us. When we do that with our life, it brings great glory and honor to His name. When God created human beings, He created them all as free moral agents. He created us so that we could make our own choices and decisions. He gave us the power and control to literally navigate the ship of our life, to take the steering wheel and drive our own life car, to be the master architect of our own destiny. This is God's tremendous gift to you—it is what separates human beings from animals—we don't live our lives by instinct. We make choices and decisions. Unlike the animal kingdom, our lives are only as routine as we make them, for we decide and choose the kind of life we are going to live. This is one of the great principles taught in the Bible, and the secret that every high achiever and successful person understands. You become what you think about most of the time! This is the way the Law of Attraction works—what you focus on becomes reality to you! The Bible says in **2 Corinthians 3:18 that whatever we behold in our lives, whatever our thoughts are constantly upon, this is what we become. By beholding we become changed!** This is one of the great success principles that many people are ignorant of in their lives. The images that you hold onto in your mind and dwell upon become reality to in your life. What you think about, what you visualize, how you talk to yourself and the words that you use, become your life!

The late Earl Nightingale from his famous training program, "Lead the Field" says this about this topic, "You see, you are, at this moment, the living embodiment of the sum total of your thoughts to this point in your life. You can be nothing else. With that in mind, five years from now, you will be the sum total of your thoughts to that point in time. But you can control your thoughts. You can decide upon that you wish to concentrate, upon what you think about from this point forward. And you become that." Remember, **Proverbs 23:7 says, "What a man thinks about in his mind, that is what he will eventually become."** That is why it is so important to be aware of your thoughts and choose them carefully, because you are the commander and chief of your world, you are the masterpiece of your own life, and you do this with your thoughts!

Chapter 5

LOA = THE LAW OF ATTRACTION

Let's begin this chapter by offering you several definitions of what this law is all about. You must be very clear on what the law is before you can learn how to use it to propel yourself to success and prosperity. Here are the five best definitions of what the **LOA** really is.

I attract to my life whatever I give my attention, energy, and focus to, whether positive or negative......

That which is like unto itself, is drawn...........

What you radiate outward in your thoughts, feelings, mental pictures, and words, you attract into your life..............

The mind is a magnet and attracts whatever corresponds to its ruling state...........................

You are a living magnet! You attract into your life people, circumstances, and situations that are in harmony with your dominant thoughts...........................

The primary principle of the **LOA** can be summed up in three basic words: **Thoughts become things!** Whatever the mind can conceive and believe, it can achieve! You see, the principle is irrefutable, whatever is going on in your mind, you are attracting into your life! You can make this universal law a power for great success and achievement. Positive, optimistic people know what they want, they know what they believe, and they have great confidence and expectation of their success, therefore they attract to themselves the predominant thoughts of their minds. Unfortunately, the reverse is true as well. Negative, pessimistic people have no idea what they want, they really do not know what they believe, and they have a bad case of victim mentality which fills their life with excuses and a lack of confidence, therefore they attract to themselves the predominant thoughts of their minds. I like what the Bible says about this in **Proverbs 10:24, "What evil people dread most will happen to them, but good people will get what they want most."** From his book, "Getting Rich Your Own Way" Brian Tracy says this about the **LOA,** "The law of attraction says that you are a living magnet. Like iron filings to a magnet, whether you have thoughts of desire or thoughts of fear, you attract people, circumstances, and events into your life that are in harmony with your dominant thoughts."

The bottom line is this: You are a living magnet!

Chapter 6

COMMON POPULAR PHRASES USED WITH THE LAW OF ATTRACTION

There is some common terminology being used today with **"The Secret"** movie and book and other **Law of Attraction** teachers and authors. Some of these terms can be confusing from a Christian perspective, while others are very clear. The goal of this chapter is to look at the common phrases used to describe the components of the **LOA.** Here are the **common phrases** frequently used for the **LOA:**

Emotional Guidance System
Creative Workshop
The Law of Deliberate Creation
The What-Is Principle
Contrast
The Law of Allowing
Vibrations or Frequency Bubble
Pre-Paving
Segment Intending

Emotional Guidance System

This is simply, good feelings or bad feelings. If you are moving toward that which you want, then you will feel positive feelings. If you are moving toward that which you do not want, then you will feel negative feelings. The premise behind this concept of the **LOA** is that how you feel determines whether you are in alignment with what you want.

This concept has some validity to it. The key to managing your emotional states is to learn to control your mental focus and to learn to control your physical body. **Emotions are created by motions!** It may have never occurred to you, but all emotion is generated by one thing–your physical body. In our live seminars we bring a man on the stage and we ask the audience to get the man depressed. They tell us he has to hang his head, frown, slump his shoulders, etc. When the man does this he looks really depressed! Then we ask the audience to notice that everything he did to get depressed happened in his physical body. It is an amazing revelation! Then we ask the audience to stand up, pick a partner and face them. Then we ask them to smile at their new partner. Then we tell them to keep smiling but tell the person how much they hate them. It is incredibly funny. No one can do it. Because the body is in a state of happiness they simply cannot get angry. This is the power of the physical body. **So, the fastest way to change your emotions is to change the way you move and use your physical body.** God gave each one of us a beautiful face, but He left it up to us to give it expression. The Bible says in **Proverbs 15 and 17 that a merry heart is like good medicine and it makes a cheerful countenance.**

The concept of deciding you are on track in your life based on your good or bad feelings, is where the challenge comes in. Gut feelings can be one indicator and sometimes right, but the Bible teaches that our personal guidance system should not be based 100% on the way we feel. There are other elements to life to be considered for personal guidance. Items such as the Holy Spirit of God. **John 16:13–14 says, "The Holy Spirit shows what is true and will come and guide you into the full truth. The Holy Spirit**

doesn't speak on His own. He will tell you only what He has heard from Jesus Christ, and He will let you know what is going to happen." And in **Psalm 119:105, the Bible says, "By your words I can see where I am going; they throw a beam of light on my dark path."** We are guided by the Holy Spirit of God, by the Word of God, by our life experiences, by role models and mentors, certain everyday events, and yes, our feelings.

The point we need to be careful on is that sometimes when you are doing what's right, or doing what's wrong, you can feel either positive or negative. I have done things in my life that I knew lined up with the Bible, I felt led by God, everything was moving in the same direction, but my initial feelings where fear, uncertainty, and insecurity. After a period of time, my feelings changed to match my values and behavior. If I had made a decision based on my feelings, I would have missed an amazing opportunity for growth and discovering further my purpose in life. That's why knowing your values, roles, your personal mission, and what's really important to you, coupled with God and His word, will help you make the right decisions when they need to be made.

Creative Workshop

This is a daily process that consists of 15–20 minute focus sessions. During this time you give thought to what you want with such clarity that your inner being responds by offering confirming emotion. In the **Book of Proverbs the Bible says, "Where there is no vision, the people perish."** This is simply a process to visualize your goals and activities for your day by reviewing your goals, thinking about what you want, and giving deep emotional input to your vision of seeing yourself achieving, succeeding, and receiving what you have been asking for. Visualization is a critical aspect to goal and dream fulfillment. Again, Brian Tracy from his book, "Getting Rich Your Own Way" says this, "Visualization is the process of creating clear mental pictures of the things that we want. Visualization activates your creative mind, triggers the **Law of Attraction,** and gives you clarity and focus in attaining your goals." This needs to be done in a relaxed and preferably quiet atmosphere. This way you can focus and concentrate better and listen to the "still small voice" of the Holy Spirit. Research has shown that if you can hold a thought or mental image for 68 seconds, it begins to materialize into form. Get a clear, crisp picture of your goal. The more frequently you can visualize your goal throughout your day, the faster your goals come to pass. Combined with emotion it will activate your subconscious mind to kick things into high gear to find ways to make this goal happen. The more clear you are about your goal, the more specific you can be, the more clear the picture gets that is sent to your brain.

Visualization in your subconscious is one of the most powerful tools in the world. However, defining what we mean by visualization is critical. We are talking about the biblical principle of **"By beholding you become changed."** You are visualizing every moment of every day. Every time you think of someone, something, a past event, a future event, Heaven— you are visualizing. Successful people visualize the kind of success they want in advance. They fill their minds with positive images. Unsuccessful people visualize their failures, problems, disappointments, and their subconscious is preprogrammed for failure.

Think about the power of this. You visualized completing school, getting your first car, meeting your husband or wife, taking a vacation, etc. Did you ever notice nearly everything you visualized actually came to pass? You visualize Heaven, meeting Jesus, seeing your loved ones who have passed away, etc. This kind of visualization is biblical, follows God's principles and creates strong motivation to bring these desires to their physical fulfillment.

The Law of Deliberate Creation

This is simply one of the eight laws of the mind, very similar to the Law of Expectation. The law of deliberate creation says that which I give thought to and that which I believe or expect...is! You get what you are thinking about, whether you want it or not. In **Matthew 15:28**, Jesus addresses a woman who had a daughter with a demon. She showed amazing faith and believed that Jesus could heal her daughter. Jesus said this to her, **"Oh, woman, your faith is something else. What you want is what you get!" Right then her daughter became well.** The **LOA** gives you what you expect. If you expect good and positive things then that's what you get, but if you expect negative, pessimistic, "I can't" things, that's exactly what you get!

The What-Is Principle

This is really a very key principle when it comes to the **LOA**. The principle is about focusing on the **"What-Is"** of your current state of being: Mentally, Emotionally, Physically, Financially, and in your Relationships. You have to put your thoughts beyond **"What-Is"** in order to attract something different or something more. We will talk about this more specifically in a later chapter.

Contrast

As it applies to the **LOA,** contrast is anything you don't like, that doesn't feel good, or causes you to be in a negative mood. We will talk about this more in the next chapter as well, it fits together perfectly with the **"What-Is"** principle. Simply put, it just means taking a look at where you are currently, then looking at where you want to go. This becomes fuel for positive thoughts and imagery which then will allow the **LOA** to occur in a faster, more intended way.

The Law of Allowing

This law says that I am that which I am, and I am willing to allow others to be that which they are. This law allows others to be who they are and make their own decisions, without trying to manipulate or control them with your perceptions, ideas, or beliefs. This law is about knowing what you want, then giving it to God, and trusting Him to bring it into your life, while allowing others to do the same. It goes back to the Bible Principle in **Romans 12:10. "Love each other with brotherly affection and take delight in honoring each other."**

Vibrations or Frequency Bubble

The word "vibe" is often used to describe a mood or feeling. Most **LOA** teachers and authors believe that every mood or feeling causes you to emit, send out, or offer a vibration, either positive or negative. Some people refer to this as "karma" or a person's "aura." To most people this sounds strange and mystical. It is often associated with eastern religion or New Age philosophy. This perception is accurate and there are some real dangers here. However, there are also someimportant biblical truths. So we don't want to throw the baby out with the bath water.

Here is an example. Have you ever had someone walk into a room and felt the atmosphere in the room change instantly? It can get tense, heavy, stressed, dark, quiet, energized, excited, or humorous. A person's attitude and inner feelings have a lot to do with that, not necessarily their energy force. A smile can literally change the atmosphere in an instant.

Let's look a bit deeper into this. Most people feel uncomfortable discussing vibration frequency. So, let's first discuss what it is. The belief is that there is a specific vibration area that surrounds your body. Each of us carries a vibration or frequency like a radio or microwave signal. Inside your bubble are all the vibrations you are sending out. Picture a force field around your body, going out maybe 2–3 feet. That would be your vibration bubble. Michael Losier from his book, "The Law of Attraction" describes it this way. "You have a bubble that is surrounding you and captured within this bubble are all the vibrations you are sending out. The Law of Attraction is responding to whatever is _**inside**_ your vibrational bubble…now that you have clarity about your desire, it's necessary to include that vibration in your current vibration because that's what the Law of Attraction responds to…It only responds to what is currently in your vibrational bubble." So everything you are talking about, complaining about, observing, praying about, and remembering are in your vibrational bubble. When people enter your bubble or get close, the energy and vibrations are then communicated to them. The way most people explain this is simple. Most of us call this our "space". You probably have said this before, "You are invading my space." This means the area around your body. We can either influence people in a positive or negative way.

But it also goes deeper. There is some truth to this proven by science. **Our entire nervous system runs on electricity.** Our cells all carry glyco-proteins which communicate with each other through electrical frequency. The hundreds of thousands of miles of neuro-pathways in our brains run on electrical frequency. When your brain is stimulated, brain cells send millions of fast-moving electrical signals along the pathways of your central nervous system. These paths are nerves that branch out into all of your muscles. Whenever you move a muscle, it is powered by electricity running through your nervous system!

In this sense, each of us do have an electrical vibration we send out. That vibration can profoundly affect you and others. We experience this in our live seminars. We can go into a seminar auditorium that is filled with negative, critical people and can literally feel the negative atmosphere, and struggle to speak the entire time. When we are done we are exhausted because the atmosphere in the seminar auditorium was so draining. Or we can go into a seminar auditorium where there is love, warmth, support, and excitement and can literally feel the positive electricity in the room. We can speak for eight hours and still feel energized!

Pre-Paving

This is the process of deliberate intent or focusing on what you want. The more deliberate you are in what you want, the less action will be needed to get unwanted things out of your experience. Let's make this simple. **Pre-paving is really a technical word for the process of repetition with focus!** This is where you concentrate and think often about what you want. A great way to anchor this focusing process is to come up with a **"desire statement."** A **desire statement** should be positive and stated with the end in mind. It's really like a positive affirmation statement except its something that you feel is going to happen or expect to happen. So you are not focusing on "What-Is" or your current situation, but on where you want to be and where you want to go with your life and how you want it to happen. A desire statement would be addressed like this:

"I am in the process of ....
"I've decided ....
"Lots can happen ....

You then fill in the blank of what you want to happen in any area of your life.

Segment Intending

This is the process of deliberate identification of what is specifically wanted for at this moment in time. Think on those things in your life that you value most at this very time. This is the opposite of multi-tasking. This is a narrow focus on one thing for a short period of time. This is about being very singular in your thought process. Being even more focused on what's really important to you, or a priority in your life, can make the segment intending more intense as well. The truth of this is that nothing comes to you unless you invite it through your thoughts.

OK, now that we have clarified some of the common popular phrases and terminology used by many authors and teachers of the **LOA**, let's move on and grow some more!

Chapter 7

WHAT YOU FOCUS ON BECOMES YOUR REALITY

Have you ever thought about this before: **Thoughts are actually things!** They are things that actually come to pass, that you can see, touch, and experience. As a matter of fact, one of the hardest concepts for many people to grasp is that they are the sole reason they are experiencing whatever they have in their lives. You are totally responsible. You are a living magnet pulling these experiences to you. Most of us attract by default, we feel we have no control over life. Our thoughts and feelings are on autopilot, so everything is just brought to us by default. This is where we begin to get into the blame and victim mentality game. We begin to blame our current life experiences on everyone and everything else. We point our fingers at others but nothing is our fault. We blame our past, our circumstances, our family, our work, our friends, our job, and our children for why our lives are not where we want them to be.

Unfortunately, most people are spending a huge amount of their thought energy and time on what they don't want and what they don't like, and then they wonder why it keeps showing up over and over again in their life. The **LOA** responds to your thoughts, whether good or bad, whether you want it or not. Because the **LOA** is a fixed, universal law, it is always working whether you believe it or understand it.

To break out of that self-defeating, negative emotion, or limiting belief, you need to stop focusing on what you don't want, or are afraid of, or trying to avoid, and start focusing on what you do want! **You need to spend 80% of your time on finding solutions to your challenges and only 20% of your time on the actual challenge itself.** People who are proactive in setting goals, and visualizing where they want to be are the successful high achievers. A **"victim mentality"** will only bring you more of the same, because you are stuck in the **"What-Is"** of life.

The Bible tells us that we get exactly what we ask for. Even though we may not verbally ask God to bring these situations, people, or circumstances into our lives, our thoughts convey to Him what we think about most of the time. Notice what King David says in the **book of Psalms 21:2, "For you have given King David his heart's desire. You did not refuse his requests! You have blessed him greatly." Chapter 145:16,19, says, "You open your hand and satisfy the desires of every living thing, He will fulfill the desires of those who honor Him. He hears their cry and saves them."**

God gives you your heart's desire. What you think about, what your dominant thoughts and mental images are, is what becomes reality to you in your life. God is not a God of force. He allows you to think upon what you want and also allows it to come into your life as well. The reality of the **LOA** is very real. **Thoughts do become things!**

Chapter 8

THE LAW OF BELIEF

The Law of Belief says that whatever you believe with conviction, becomes your reality. That which a person gives thought to and that which you believe or expect...**IS!** You get what you are thinking about most of the time, whether you want it or not. I like what Norman Vincent Peale said in his book, "Why Some Positive Thinkers Get Powerful Results". "When things are not going well for you, ask yourself whether you are thinking good things or bad. It is a well established fact that there is a strong tendency for outward manifestations to match inner thought patterns. The thoughts, ideas, and concepts that lodge into our minds result in attitudes and beliefs, and these in turn determine whether we experience failure or success." So the principle here is that if you are thinking negative and pessimistic things, they tend to become a physical reality to you in your life. The same happens when you think positive, optimistic, and empowering thoughts.

The Bible has a lot to say about the Law of Belief. In a story in the Bible, a Roman Centurion, a man of great power and influence, came up to Jesus and inquired of Him. The man had a servant whom he loved who was near death with a sickness. This man of power and influence came to Jesus believing that He could do something to improve his servant's situation. This account is found in **Matthew 8:5–13.** Notice what Jesus said to him, **"Then Jesus said to the Centurion, Go! It will be done just as you have believed it would. Right then his servant**

was healed." In another place, a father brought a de-mon-possessed boy to Jesus and asked Him to heal the boy "**If**" it was possible. This account is found in **Mark 9:14–26.** Notice what Jesus says to the father, **"Jesus said, If? There are no 'Ifs' among believers. Anything is possible for someone who believes.**" You need to believe that God wants to do great and awe-some things in your life, but you must believe and have faith to see it become reality. You cannot talk faith and belief, but then think doubtful or pessimis-tic thoughts. **You have to believe!**

Your beliefs about everything are like absolute commands that rule you. In your life your beliefs tell you how things are, what is possible, and what is impossible. They tell you what you can and can-not do. Your beliefs shape every single action, ev-ery thought, and every feeling you experience. Most people never even question their long held beliefs. If you ever wonder why people do the foolish things they do, you can know their actions are simply the result of their deeply rooted beliefs.

It is important for you to understand that your beliefs have the power to create, and the power to destroy. God gave you the awesome ability to take any experience in your life, and create a belief for it. That belief can totally destroy your life, or you can create a belief that will literally save and enrich your life! Once accepted, your belief becomes an unquestioned command to your nervous system. And that belief has the power to increase, or limit the possibilities of your life.

Chapter 9

WHERE'S YOUR FOCUS: PRESENT OR FUTURE?

Let's touch briefly upon how the **"What-Is"** principle goes together with the concept of Contrast. As you remember, the **"What-Is"** of your life is your current situation in every aspect of your life, physically, financially, emotionally, mentally, spiritually, and in your relationships. It is your life right now! The only way to change your life and your current situation is to stop thinking about your current state if you are going to attract and bring other life changing opportunities, people and situations into your life. Remember, the **LOA** only responds to your dominant thoughts. So whatever current thoughts you are focusing on, the **LOA** is going to give you more of the same.

The key is to shift your paradigm, the way you look at things. You have to change your thinking! Stop looking at your finances, your health, your job, your relationships, and your environment as it is now. Start visualizing each as you want them to be.

Some of you might be asking, "How do I know, or how will I know, if I am focusing on the "What-Is" of my life or my current situation?"

This is where you have to pay attention to your physical body and your mental world. If you are feeling stressed, worried, fearful, overwhelmed, out of control, physically sick, depressed, unmotivated, scared, and living with no hope, you are more than likely focusing on the **"What-Is"** of your life and operating on your own and not asking for help. Reverse this and claim God's promises for victory. Read comforting Bible promises. Listen to the Holy Spirit of God. Think positive and hopeful thoughts about your future. Believe and have faith that God, people, circumstances, and situations that are in your life are moving you to the abundant life God promised. **Keep reminding yourself that thoughts become things!**

Another way to really help you in this process of controlling what you focus on, is the concept of **contrast. Contrast** simply is taking an honest and responsible look at where you are right now, then comparing that to where you want to be and where you want to go with your life. The one thing **contrasting** does for you is provide clarity on what you don't want. This then helps us answer the question, **"What do I really want in every aspect of my life?"** It is important to focus on what you don't want just long enough to bring clarity about what it is that you do want! Then focus your thoughts and visual images upon those things and let it happen!

Chapter 10

COOPERATE WITH GOD AND ALLOW HIM

This is where the **Law of Allowing** comes into play with the **LOA.** This is where you claim God's blessing to bring into your life what He promises. God allows us to choose our destiny here and hereafter. You believe you are deserving of living an abundant life because you are made in His image. You are nature's greatest miracle in creation. God wants His created beings to accomplish their goals and dreams in conjunction with the principles and laws He has for them, but, He allows us to choose our destiny and does not interfere with our choices.

Here's how it works. When you choose your destiny, your career, marriage, goals, children, and future, you follow God's principles. Then you trust God, you put it into His hands, and know He will bring your request to reality. The **"allowing process"** is simply God allowing you to make your own choices and you allowing God to work through that choice. He lays before you blessings and curses. Do what He says and you will reap the blessings. Disobey and you will reap the painful consequences. When you have made a choice in harmony with God's principles, then you claim God's promise to bring it into your life. You believe you are deserving and that God has no limitations, He can do all things. This is where the law of cause and effect comes into your life, that you will reap whatever you have sown.

Psalm 37:4–5 says, "Do what the Lord wants, and He will give you your heart's desire. Let the Lord lead you and trust Him to help."

The process of allowing is stepping out of the way and letting God be God! He is Alpha and Omega. He knows everything. Do it His way! **Proverbs 3:5–6 says, "Trust in the Lord with all your heart and not in your own judgment. Always let Him lead you, and He will clear the road for you to follow."** It is important in this allowing process to be 100% positive—have 100% faith—100% believing that God knows what He is doing and will take care of everything to make it happen in your life.

You see, we meet thousands of people who did not follow God's principles, or laws. They are physically and emotionally sick, on anti-depressant drugs, they are bankrupt morally, addicted to alcohol, tobacco and drugs, and are controlled by the cable and satellite TV industry and the fast food industry. Most have zero spiritual life, their marriages are on the rocks, and their finances are a disaster. They live in poverty, fear, and hopelessness. **Why?** Because they did not **"allow"** God's process in their life. So, they are reaping the results.

Let me give you a powerful example of this. There is a church in Albany, Georgia by the name of Sherwood Baptist Church. This church has a set of brothers, Alex and Stephen Kendrick, and a pastor who had a vision for creating powerful Christian movies with a message. Hence, the movie, "Facing the Giants" was birthed into existence. This movie is the perfect example of the Law of Attraction at work. You have a football coach and his wife, a school, and a football team who get into a spiritual rut. They are focused too much on what's not going right, what they don't have, losing, having a victim mentality, negative thinking, and God is not really first in their lives. They use phrases such as "Why does this always happen to me?", "I hate this car!", "Like everything else, its my fault.", "Why is God doing this to me?", and "Why is this so hard?" Remember, people reap what they sow and the dominant thoughts of a person become physical reality to them. If you want a miserable life, talk miserable talk, think miserable thoughts, the **Law of Attraction** will give you exactly what you ask for. Then by God's grace, a miracle happens. Coach Grant Taylor feels his life has reached rock bottom so he decides to turn to God's Word for answers and encouragement. The Holy Spirit touches his heart and mind and he begins to see God's will revealed to him through the Bible. This experience begins to birth a powerful revival in his life, the football team, and in the school. What happens next is the key to the **"allowing"** process. Instead of God being on the back burner or in the back seat of their lives, He now became first priority and they allowed Him to drive their lives. Here is a quote from Coach Taylor as he is speaking to his football team during the preparation for an upcoming football game. This really sums up how the **LOA** works in our lives for good.

"We have to give God our best in every area of our lives. If we win, we praise Him for it. If we lose, we will still praise Him. Either way, we honor Him with our activities and attitudes. God's blessings follow those who honor Him."

Just this shift in attitude and thinking changed everything. Coach Taylor got a new truck given to him, he got a raise, the football team began to win again, what appeared to be a problem became a challenge, and they accepted responsibility for their lives. The football players began to believe in themselves as winners, relationships between students and parents became better, and true divine miracles began to happen in many areas of their lives. **All be-**

cause they put God first. They made a commitment to live by God's Biblical principles and then **"allow"** God to move in their lives.

Instead of trying to do everything on their own they cooperated with Him and the **LOA** worked in a positive and mighty way. Their values and beliefs were in alignment with their behavior and so they experienced inner peace and a spiritual relationship with God.

So, the **"Law of Allowing"** is when a person reads and lives by God's word and they follow God's principles and God's laws. They stand on the promises and by faith go forward in reaching for their dreams and goals. Then they choose to trust in God to bring to them their requests, their desires, and their needs.

Chapter 11

THREE STEPS TO GETTING WHAT YOU WANT

In the sales profession you are taught that when all is said and done, you have to ask for the sale! Nobody is really going to pull out their checkbook and say to you, "Hey, I really feel like writing you a $1,000 check. Is there any way I can write a larger one?" We all know this just doesn't happen. The key principle in the sales process is: You have to ask to get! The same goes for igniting the **LOA** process and getting to the allowing stage. There are three basic steps that you need to follow to activate the **LOA** in your life....

ASK...... BELIEVE...... RECEIVE!

So, step #1 is to ASK! This is where you put into action the answer to the question: "What do you really want out of life?" Once you know the answers to that question and it is crystal clear in your mind, then you ask God to bring them into your life. There are several important points to understand in the asking process.

The first thing is you need to ask as if you expect to get it. This is where the Law of Expectation really kicks into high gear! Your level of expectation will affect everything in your life, from your attitude, your body language, your eye contact, your tone of voice, and your choice of words. You need to ask with a positive expectation because we tend to get exactly what we expect. The Bible says in **Matthew**

7:7, "Ask and you shall receive. Search and you will find. Knock, and the door will be opened to you." Ask with conviction, see what you are asking for the way you want it to be. In **John 16:23–24 the Bible says, "Ask in my name then it will be given to you, so that you will be completely happy."**

And in **1 John 3:22 the Bible says, "God will give us whatever we ask for, because we obey Him and do what pleases Him."**

The next thing is you need to ask in a very specific manner. You make your requests known to God. Be very specific and focus on what you do want and not on what you don't want!

Next, you need to ask with a deep sense of passion and emotion.

The last thing is to ask repeatedly. Ask over and over again, pray without ceasing as the Bible says. Just because a door closes or an opportunity goes away, doesn't mean that what your asking for will not come to you. It just means not here, not now, not yet! You can't waiver. **James 1:5–7 says,**

"If any of you lack wisdom, let his ask of God who gives to all men liberally...and it shall be given him. But let him ask in faith, nothing wavering. For he that wavereth is like the wave of the sea driven with the wind and tossed. For let not that man think he shall receive anything of the Lord."

The next step, step #2 is to BELIEVE! The Bible clearly states in **Matthew 21:22, "Whatever things you ask for in prayer, believing, you will receive them."** Jack Canfield from his book, "The Success Principles" has a great idea on how you can really activate this step in the **LOA** process. It's called the **"AS-IF"** principle. He says this, "One of the great strategies for success is to act **"AS-IF"** you are already where you want to be. The Law of Attraction simply states that like attracts like. The more you create the feelings of already having something, the faster you attract it to you."

I have a great real life illustration of the **"AS-IF"** principle that many of you may not be aware of. It is the story of one of my favorite golfers, Fred Couples. Fred is from the Redmond, WA area, and his best friend, CBS sports announcer, is Jim Nantz. Fred Couples and Jim Nantz were college roommates in the late 1970s at the University of Houston. Both of them grew up with a great love for golf.

Fred Couples had the dream from a young age of winning the Master's golf tournament. Jim Nantz had the dream of becoming a CBS sports announcer. They used to play act You together, that Fred won the Master's golf title and that Jim would interview Fred in the green room in Butler Cabin where the winner receives the green jacket from the previous year's winner. They are then interviewed by a CBS sports announcer for national television. They did this frequently, they talked about it, they visualized it, they believed that event would happen to both of them one day. Amazingly, fourteen years later, in 1992, the scene they had rehearsed over and over again in Taub Hall at the University of Houston played out in reality as the whole world was watching. Fred Couples won the Master's title and was taken by tournament officials to the famous Butler Cabin where he was interviewed by none other than CBS sports announcer, his dear and close friend, Jim Nantz. After the camera's stopped rolling, the two embraced one another with tears of joy in their eyes. They always knew it was going to be the Master's tournament that Fred Couples would win and that Jim Nantz would be there to cover it for CBS. This is an amazing and true life experience of how powerful the **"AS-IF"** principle can be in our lives.

So start now and **BE** who you want to be. Start now and **DO** the actions that go along with being that person, and soon you will find that you easily **HAVE** everything you want in life. Health, wealth, and fulfilling relationships, you can have those for your life. I believe that if you go there in the mind first, then you can make it manifest into physical reality. The great Michael Jordan said when asked about his basketball greatness, "I visualized where I wanted to be, what kind of player I wanted to become. I knew exactly where I wanted to go, and I focused on getting there." And as Paul Harvey would say, "we all know the rest of the story on that one!" Today almost all world-class athletes and other peak performers are powerful at visualization. They see it, they feel it, they experience it before they actually do it. They begin as Stephen Covey would say, "with the end in mind."

You see, your subconscious mind is responsible for your long-term success, failure, or mediocrity. It is responsible for coordinating and generating every element of your thinking, feeling, speaking, and acting. The great news is that your 52 mind works on the instructions it is given. It is the images that are dwelt upon consciously and repeatedly that get absorbed like a sponge onto the mental software of the subconscious mind. All successful and high achieving individuals train their minds to think about what they want in their lives, what type of person they want to become, they constantly think about their goals and dreams, they think about their values and the things that are really important to them. The amazing thing about the subconscious mind is that it is incapable of distinguishing between an actual event and one that is only imagined. Do you see the power in this for your life? Through repeated visualization, you can literally convince your subconscious mind that a desired goal or event has already taken place or has been accomplished. Then, once your mind believes something to be true, it automatically adjusts your thoughts, words, emotions, and behaviors to be consistent with that of your visualization. Your mind and body interpret your visual images as reality and respond to your visualizations as though they were already happening. Rich has a great example of this in his own personal life.

He had a very real experience with this concept during his college days in Wenatchee, WA. He was attending Wenatchee Valley College, which at the time offered a AAA degree in Ski Instruction and Coaching. How many people do you know who have a college degree in skiing? Anyway, he thought he was a good skier when he arrived there, but after seeing the other students in the program, he realized real fast his opinion of himself was very over-inflated. He was average at best and knew he had to work very hard to get to the level of a Full Certified ski instructor. It was then he was introduced to a tool that changed the direction of his skiing life forever. It was called *SyberVision.* Basically it was a muscle memory program created specifically for skiing with the science and technology of the Stanford Neuropsychology Research Laboratory. The video was of two skiers who have perfect mechanics and skiing form, and they are professional ski instructors and race coaches. He would watch it everyday in the morning for one hour. The results were frankly amazing. In two years, his skiing accelerated in a visual image to look very similar to the skiers he was watching on the video. You see, he was not that good of a skier at first, but he watched the video everyday and imagined, thought, and spoke words of what he wanted to look like. And just like he desired, his subconscious mind had an image of what he wanted to be like, and it worked everyday to make that happen. At the end of two years, he received the ski instructor of the year award, he was asked to be the Assistant Ski School Director for a Washington ski area, and he was a Full-Certified ski instructor as well. He is a living, breathing example that if you go there in the mind first, then it will become a physical reality to you.

What the mind can conceive and believe, it can achieve!

In **Matthew Chapter 9:20–22,** a very sick woman who had been hemorrhaging for twelve years came to Jesus and knew if she could just touch His robe, she could be healed. Here is what Jesus said to her, **"Don't worry! You are now well because of your faith. At that moment she was healed."** It is so absolutely obvious in the Bible, the things we want, whether they be material, physical, mental, emotional, or financial, you receive what you ask for only by faith! Jesus healed many people, and the most common word He used with them becoming well was **"your faith has made you well....or because you have believed it shall be done unto you!"**

And finally, the last step, Step #3 is RECEIVING! One thing that is very important in this step is to know that with God all things are possible! If God is for us, then who can possibly be against us? When we partner with God, the power of the universe is literally unleashed, the Creator of the universe releases power into our lives to allow us to do more, be more, and have more than we could ever do on our own. This is part of the allowing process. Be clear and specific on what it is that you want. Make sure it is in harmony with God's laws and principles, then get out of the way, and see the power of cooperating with God manifest itself in you life. Let God orchestrate and open up new doors you would have never thought possible. You don't need to know the beginning from the end. Just do what He says and your success is guaranteed! Part of faith is to know that God is big enough, God is in control enough, and has a master plan, all you need to do is **Ask, Believe, and Receive!**

CONCLUSION

So what's so secret about **"The Secret?"** What's the secret behind **"The Secret?"** The logical and biblical conclusion we draw from this is that there is *no secret*! It's a truth that's been taught in the Bible for thousands of years. We hope this book has been beneficial to you in **decoding "The Secret"** and showing you a balanced and beneficial approach to the **Law of Attraction.** We see too many people today living mediocre and average lives because they do not understand the power of their own minds and how the subconscious mind really works. Many do not understand that the **LOA** is affecting their lives every moment they still breathe.

Most people today are making a living rather than living a great life....

Most people today are focusing on trials and problems rather than being grateful and having a heart of gratitude for everything they have.........

Most people today are focusing on being discouraged and defeated rather than living life with a positive, enthusiastic attitude.........

Most people today are wandering aimlessly through life rather than having a purpose and reaching for their goals and dreams.........

What most people do not realize is that they have chosen that type of life and the **Law of Attraction** gives them what they think about and what they focus on. God isn't going to force Himself upon you. So if you make poor choices and decisions with your life, He allows the consequences of those decisions to take their course. You cannot just hope for success and wish it to appear magically or by osmosis. **We believe and teach that success in this life is a planned event, it doesn't just happen.** You have to decide what you want out of life and then create a plan to achieve it and then go after it with a passion and desire so great nothing can stop you.

Most people never decide what they want out of life. They let everyone and everything else do it because they never decide they are out of control physically, mentally, emotionally, spiritually and financially. The greatest tragedy is that when we don't decide what we want, we end up settling for far less than we are capable of. As we have said before, the Bible states, "you will reap what you sow." This is the Law of Cause and Effect. It is alive and well today. You are a living magnet, whether you believe it or whether you accept it or not. It is a universal fact of life. Everything you think, see, speak, your attitude, and associations—all work together to pull and attract into our lives things that bring thoughts to reality. We want to encourage you to decide what it is that you really don't want out of life, then crystallize what it is that you do want. You need to clear all negative and limiting beliefs out of your mind and spend time every day visualizing and feeling what you want to have, do, and be. Trust in God to answer your prayers and allow Him to bring it to you.

Begin by taking responsibility for your life. Get out of a victim mentality. Choose to have a positive attitude, a vision and purpose to live for. Have a giving and grateful heart, and take action. Ultimately, it's not about quantum physics or some energy force out in space, but basic common sense and cooperating with God and His principles of life.

So get out there and create the life of your dreams, and remember, that **the only limits you have in life are the one's you put on yourself!** Take charge of your life and get out there and live a life of all power and no limits!

For additional information go to:
www.BiblicalLawOfAttraction.com

Making a defining difference in your life...

Now available

LIVING AND APPLYING THE
LAW OF ATTRACTION STUDY GUIDE

Set yourself apart!

Rise to the top by exercising your ability to apply the Law of Attraction to your life and make it part of your daily habits and decision-making.

Make the Law of Attraction Part of Your Day-to-Day Life!

Now that you know about the Law of Attraction, it is time to apply it! Rich Cavaness and Leo Schreven have created a new resource to aid you with your Bible study and discussions with church members, friends, co-workers, and family, in an easy to apply study guide format.

This resource, *Living and Applying the Law of Attraction*, will help you and your discussion groups to:

- **Learn the practical and relevant application of the Law of Attraction to change your life forever!**
- **Create a new and exciting mindset for your life...........**
- **Live your life cooperating and trusting in God..............**
- **Incorporate the principles of success into your lifestyle.....**

To order study guides, please call: 1-888-811-5663 or if ordering large quantities please call the publisher directly at 1-518-358-3494

Law of Attraction Resources

*For _FREE_ 10 minute Video clip
*E-Book of Decoding The Secret
• DVD of the Law of Attraction
• CD of the Law of Attraction

Go to
www.BiblicalLawOfAttraction.com

To order the *Decoding The Secret: The Law of Attraction from a Biblical Perspective* book, please call or e-mail:

1-888-811-5663
info@allpowerseminar.com

For large orders, please call
1-518-358-3494

MORE RESOURCES

Both Rich Cavaness and Leo Schreven are available for:

- keynote addresses
- business training
- church seminars
- community motivational conferences.

Topics include:

All Power (weekend) Conference
Living a No Limits Life (one day) Conference
Law of Attraction (one day) Conference
Israel in Prophecy (weekend) Conference
Revelation and End Times (10 day) Prophecy Conference
Finding Balance in an Out of Balance World (one day)
   Conference

For Seminar or Ministry Information
Check out our website: www.allpowerseminar.com

For products, seminar availability and information please contact:

Email: info@allpowerseminar.com
Phone: 1-888-811-5663

All Power Seminars
PO Box 579
Kettle Falls, WA 99141

All Power Ministries
PO Box 1158
Kettle Falls, WA 99141

Rich Cavaness e-mail: rich_cavaness@msn.com

Leo Schreven e-mail: allpowerseminar@cs.com

All Power Personal Development and Coaching Network

This is the most revolutionary and thorough coaching system in the marketplace today!

Our opportunity is simple and we offer three main benefits:

- Master your life in 60 days All Power Coaching System
- Membership in a 12 month personal development network
- A direct market plan that can make you unlimited income!

Not only will Rich and Leo train, teach, and coach you but so will some of the best role models in the personal development industry such as: **John Maxwell, Jack Canfield, Robert Kiyosaki, Robert Allen, Brian Tracy, Stephen Covey, Dale Carnegie, Harv Eker, and Rick Warren.** Each month one of these powerful and educated individuals will lend their expertise to help take your life to the next level of success and achievement by reading one of their books! We coach you through our 60 day system, weekly e-mails and end of month conference calls.

Success leaves clues, come learn from the best!

Check out our website: www.allpowernetwork.com

Call toll free: 1-877-250-7697

Living a No Limits Life Today!
Pre-Release Information

*E-Book of Living a No Limits Life Today

**Go to
www.BiblicalLawOfAttraction.com**

To order the *Living a No Limits Life Today: 16 Life Changing Principles for Gaining Control, Balance, Power and Success in Your Life* book, please call or email:

**1-888-811-5663
info@allpowerseminar.com**

ABOUT THE AUTHORS

Rich Cavaness has a passion for writing and teaching on the subject of personal development and motivation. His discovery and application in his personal and business life of the Law of Attraction has allowed him to live his life with all power and no limits. Rich has been married to his wife, Heather, for 20 years—they have two children, Sarah and Jonathan. He has more life experience at 40 years of age than most people acquire in a lifetime. He has been a professional ski instructor, a 17-year entrepreneur, an evangelist, a pastor, a coach, an avid network marketer, an author, a health and wellness industry advocate, and real estate investor. He has been an employee, an employer, a sales person, a laborer, a custodian, and a coordinator and leader of people. He is currently the co-founder with Leo Schreven of the the global personal development and coaching company, All Power Network. Also, he is the current President and Director/Speaker for All Power Ministries and owns and operates a wellness and financial education company "Personal Wellness Solutions", LLC. His passion is teaching and helping people improve their lives by understanding the power of the Law of Attraction and the other universal laws of the mind. He teaches people today how to master the important areas of their lives: physical, mental, emotional, spiritual, financial, and relational. When he isn't speaking, coaching, or teaching, Rich loves the outdoors, loves to ski, exercise, and be anywhere there are big mountains and pine trees. He values time and fun activities with his family. The Cavaness family currently make their home in Charleston, West Virginia.

Leo Schreven has more energy than the energizer bunny! Leo lives his life with endless possibilities and passion. His world-wide speaking schedule keeps him busy. Known as the "machine gun speaker" his unique speed and power combined with continuous humor keeps audiences on the edge of their seats. He has many titles but is best known as an ordained minister, a businessman, author, and TV personality. His accomplishments in dozens of areas are too many to name. Yet under all the success is a very simple man who donates his time and money to dozens of humanitarian projects. Leo loves nothing more than the quiet life of coming home to his ranch in Washington to his lovely wife and daughter. He is most happy when he is enjoying the great outdoors, hunting and fishing. Leo is as much at home in front of an audience of 10,000 as he is a small audience of a dozen. He is a cowboy at heart, and is most comfortable alone with his family or in the wilds of Alaska with his best friend Keith. Leo's enthusiasm and motivation has inspired thousands to new heights in their lives. He has collaborated with Rich to produce this book as part of the All Power Personal Development and Coaching Network.

REFERENCES AND ENDNOTES

Byrne, Rhonda *The Secret*
Prime Time Production, 2006

Adler, Jerry *Newsweek Magazine, "Decoding the Secret"*
March 5, 2007 issue

Losier, Michael J. *Law of Attraction*
Michael J. Losier Publisher, 2006

McGhee, Paul PhD. *Health, Healing and Amuse System: Humor as Survival Training*
Humor Your Tumor Column, July 1999

Hill, Napoleon *Think and Grow Rich*
Renaissance Books, 2001

Peale, Norman Vincent *Why Some Positive Thinkers Get Powerful Results*
Ballantine Books, 1986

Hicks, Esther and Jerry *The Law of Attraction*
Hay House Inc. 2006

Doyle, Bob *Wealth Beyond Reason*
Trafford Publishing, 2003

Vitale, Joe *The Attractor Factor*
John Wiley and Sons, Inc. 2005

Canfield, Jack and Hansen, Mark Victor *The Aladdin Factor*
The Berkley Publishing Group, 1995

Canfield, Jack *The Success Principles*
Harper Collins Publishers, 2005

Rosenbaum, Ernest H. MD and Isadora R. MA
Attitude: The Will to Live Article
Coping with Cancer, Published, April 1999

Tracy, Brian *Getting Rich Your Own Way*
John Wiley and Sons, Inc. 2004

Tracy, Brian *Million Dollar Habits*
Entrepreneur Media Inc. 2004

Gikandi, David Cameron *A Happy Pocket Full of Money*
Images of One Publishing, 2002

Kiplinger Magazine, "Escape the Credit Card Trap"
October 2005

Money Magazine, December 2005 article, Pg. 94

Bible References

Peterson, Eugene *The Message*
NavPress Publishing Group 1993-1995

Contemporary English Version
American Bible Society 1995

The Answer, New Century Version
Thomas Nelson Publishing 2003

New King James Version
Thomas Nelson Publishing 1997

King James Version
Thomas Nelson Publishing 1976

New International Version
Zondervan Bible Publishers 1978

Living Bible Paraphrase
Kenneth N. Taylor 1971